Geek out!

A MODERN NERD'S GUIDE TO

STEAMPUNK

BY NICOLE HORNING

Gareth Stevens
PUBLISHING

Please visit our website, www.garethstevens.com. For a free color catalog of all our high-quality books, call toll free 1-800-542-2595 or fax 1-877-542-2596.

Cataloging-in-Publication Data

Names: Horning, Nicole.
Title: A modern nerd's guide to steampunk / Nicole Horning.
Description: New York : Gareth Stevens Publishing, 2020. | Series: Geek out! | Includes glossary and index.
Identifiers: ISBN 9781538240267(pbk.) | ISBN 9781538240281 (library bound) | ISBN 9781538240274 (6 pack)
Subjects: LCSH: Steampunk culture–Juvenile literature.
Classification: LCC PN3448.S73 H67 2020 | DDC 700'.411–dc23

First Edition

Published in 2020 by
Gareth Stevens Publishing
111 East 14th Street, Suite 349
New York, NY 10003

Copyright © 2020 Gareth Stevens Publishing

Designer: Sarah Liddell
Editor: Abby Badach Doyle

Photo credits: Cover, p. 1 CREATISTA/Shutterstock.com; texture used throughout StrelaStudio/Shutterstock.com; p. 5 Christopher Furlong/Staff/Getty Images News/Getty Images; p. 7 Universal History Archive/Contributor/ Universal Images Group/Getty Images; p. 8 Ellerslie/Shutterstock.com; p. 9 superjoseph/Shutterstock.com; pp. 12, 13 Adam Berry/Stringer/Getty Images News/Getty Images; p. 15 Slick-o-bot/Wikimedia Commons; p. 17 Araya Diaz/Contributor/Getty Images Entertainment/Getty Images; p. 18 OZMedia/Shutterstock.com; p. 21 Gitanna/Shutterstock.com; p. 22 Alex Tihonovs/Shutterstock.com; pp. 23, 24 NurPhoto/Contributor/NurPhoto/ Getty Images; p. 25 thekovtun/Shutterstock.com; p. 27 Albert L. Ortega/Contributor/Getty Images Entertainment/ Getty Images; p. 29 Helen H. Richardson/Contributor/Denver Post/Getty Images.

Printed in the United States of America

CPSIA compliance information: Batch #CS19GS: For further information contact Gareth Stevens, New York, New York at 1-800-542-2595.

CONTENTS

Words in the glossary appear in **bold** type the first time they are used in the text.

WHAT IS STEAMPUNK?

Do you like history, technology, and costumes? Then you might love steampunk! Steampunk is a type of **science fiction** that imagines what people in the past would have thought the future looked like. At the center of steampunk are real or imagined steam-powered machines from the 1800s. Steampunk fans mix old and new things to create a new world.

Today's fans got inspiration from books that were written many years earlier. Then, steampunk started showing up in movies, at **conventions**, and in fashion. It has even crossed over into music, games, and miniatures, or tiny things.

THE NERD COMMUNITY

A nerd or a geek is someone who deeply **appreciates** something. They may go to events with other fans, dress up, or read books and watch movies about the thing that they love. Geek **culture** is about sharing interests with a group of people and being a part of that community.

Steampunk often takes something
from history, such as clothing, and combines
it with something that is new, such
as parts of machines.

HISTORY OF STEAMPUNK

Steampunk is a smaller part of culture, called a subculture. It became a trend in the 1990s and grew more popular in the 2000s. This **fascinating** subculture combines new technology with things from the past, especially the Victorian Age. The Victorian Age, named for Queen Victoria who reigned at the time, took place from the 1830s to the 1900s in the United Kingdom.

Many inventions, including the telephone, were created during the Victorian Age. Bicycles also became popular. The clothing people wore changed, too. For example, women's dresses had narrow sleeves and large, full skirts. Steampunk is inspired by the clothing from this time.

CREATION OF STEAMPUNK

It's believed that author K. W. Jeter created the term "steampunk" in the 1980s. He was writing science fiction books that took place during the Victorian Age, and he wanted to separate the books he was writing from other authors' styles.

Paintings, drawings, and photos from Victorian times show us what fashion looked like back then. What surprises you about the way people dressed?

THE STEAMPUNK AIRSHIP

Society changed a lot in the Victorian Age. Steam power created mighty machines. There were developments in science, too. During this time, Victorians imagined flying machines, such as airships, and underwater machines, such as submarines. However, what the Victorians thought of was different than what was later created!

Because these things were first dreamed of during this time, airships and submarines are popular images in steampunk. People who like steampunk may imagine what it would be like if the Victorians actually created these things. Then, they may add that into their character or story. For example, someone's steampunk **persona** could be a pilot, captain, inventor, or mechanic.

The airship is a popular image in steampunk. Some fans pretend to be airship pirates, who attack and steal ships in the sky!

8

OAMARU, NEW ZEALAND

Oamaru is a town in New Zealand that has buildings with a steampunk theme. Many of the people who live there also enjoy steampunk. They even have steampunk parades! Some residents wear costumes all the time. Some people moved to the town just so they could be close to other steampunk fans.

GETTING STARTED

The first thing to do when getting started in the steampunk community is to think about your persona, or a particular way to look, behave, and talk. You can create your character, pick a special name, and a job. Do you want to be a scientist? An adventurer? A pirate? If you always wanted to be something else, you can create that in your steampunk persona!

You don't need to be a scientist, adventurer, or pirate to be in steampunk, though! You can create any kind of character you want. If you do create a persona, it's good to make sure everything you do matches.

JUST BE YOU!

You don't need a persona in order to enjoy steampunk. Many fans are involved in steampunk without creating a character. A persona may make it more fun and have more meaning for you, but the important thing is to just have fun and be creative with it!

THE STEAMPUNK PERSONA

- WHAT AM I EXCITED TO PRETEND TO BE?

- WHAT DO I WANT MY CHARACTER TO DO?
SHOULD IT BE A PIRATE, A SCIENTIST,
AN ADVENTURER, A CAPTAIN, A PILOT,
OR SOMETHING ELSE?

- WHAT CLOTHING DOES THIS CHARACTER
NEED THAT MATCHES WHAT IT DOES?

- WHAT GADGETS DOES THIS CHARACTER
NEED FOR WHAT IT DOES?

- HOW DOES THIS CHARACTER ACT?

- HOW DOES THIS CHARACTER TALK?

- DOES THIS CHARACTER HAVE
A DIFFERENT NAME?

Creating a steampunk persona might
take a lot of time. Think about these questions
to help create your character!

When you're making your persona and deciding what to wear, make sure everything goes together. Your clothing and gadgets should match the type of character you are. For example, if you're a scientist, you might have a lab coat. An airship pilot might have goggles to help see far distances when flying.

You also should make sure how your character acts and talks matches how it looks and what it does. A certain character might react differently to a situation than another character. For example, a mischievous pirate would act differently than a rich nobleman.

Some families like to dress up and make steampunk characters together!

TEA PARTIES AND TIME TRAVELERS

In the early days of steampunk, people would dress up in their full costume and get together with other fans at time travelers' events or at tea parties. These events allowed them to meet others who liked the same things, especially in the early days of steampunk when fewer people knew about it.

13

CREATING YOUR STEAMPUNK LOOK

Clothing is one of the most important parts of steampunk. Fans spend a lot of time creating their character's look. First, start with the basics like a coat, shirt, and pants or a dress. Then, add other decorations and pieces on top.

For costume inspiration, look at pictures in a steampunk book or on a website. You can even get ideas from people you meet at steampunk gatherings or events. It's okay to borrow someone else's idea, but don't copy them exactly! You want to make sure that you're making your own character that reflects your individual creative thinking.

OLD MEETS NEW

Steampunk generally borrows inspiration from the Victorian Age, but you don't have to dress in clothing from this era if you don't want to. Steampunk is also about combining history with new items. If there's a different time period that inspires you, go for it! The biggest part of steampunk is having fun.

Some steampunk fans start with a simple costume. Then, they leave room to add little details later, like flowers, machine parts, or jewelry.

15

Once you have the dress or coat set that you want to wear, you can then get really creative! You can add buttons, cogs, or even clock pieces to your clothes.

One of the common clothing items in steampunk is the top hat. People will often add clock pieces, feathers, and goggles to their top hat. Sometimes, the hat will be simple and have only goggles on it. Other hats are really creative and have a lot of pieces added to them, like little figurines (small models) or doctor's tools. Some hats may even have small clocks on them!

COGS

Cogs are metal wheels with ridges that look like teeth. They help power machines and are often used in people's steampunk looks. However, these little metal pieces aren't necessary unless you really want them in your look. Some people prefer to only add cogs to machines they carry with them.

People will often decorate their hat as much as they do the rest of their costume!

17

WHERE TO FIND STEAMPUNK GEAR

There are many items, like cogs and goggles, that are common in steampunk costumes. However, that doesn't mean that they're needed in every look. Fans can use any item that inspires them.

Steampunk costumes aren't about copying something exactly, such as dressing up like your favorite superhero. Steampunk is more of a general feeling. That means picking what items you want for your look can feel **overwhelming**. The good news is there are plenty of places to find pieces to create your look. You might not even plan on finding an item, but end up seeing something you like at a store or convention!

Items to add to your steampunk look can be found anywhere! Steampunk allows you to be creative and use any items that you find in stores or around your home as part of your look.

PUTTING TOGETHER YOUR STEAMPUNK LOOK

- ETSY
- EBAY
- STEAMPUNK CONVENTIONS
- STEAMPUNK WEBSITES
- THRIFT STORES
- CRAFT SHOWS

JEWELRY

Jewelry can help complete your look. A pocket watch is a small, fun item that can be useful and make your costume look great! Some people who make jewelry might give it a steampunk look by adding cogs to it. They might make jewelry out of items they find around the house or at yard sales!

19

Conventions are a good place to get ideas for your steampunk look. You can also buy items there. Conventions will often have **vendors** set up where you can get a hat, goggles, cogs, and more.

While conventions are fun, the best place to start is thrift stores. These stores have items that others don't want or need anymore. The best part? Prices are cheap! Thrift stores can help you find either the old or new pieces of your costume. For example, you don't have to use the whole shirt you buy—you can take off the buttons and add them to something else!

START AT HOME!

Before you buy anything new, it's a good idea to first check around your home for things that your parents or guardians don't need anymore. Always ask them first! This is especially important because that item may be cut, glued, or painted and won't be able to be used again.

If you buy an old watch at a thrift store, you can take it apart to add the cogs and other pieces to **modify** your costume.

STEAMPUNK DIY

Dressing up is the most important part of steampunk, but the fun doesn't stop at costumes! You can also make items to display in your room, like bookends or a hook for your wall. These items can be sold at conventions. Arts and crafts activities are often called DIY, or do-it-yourself, projects.

Steampunk mostly combines old and new things. Some people change everyday objects to look steampunk. For example, they might add cogs to a lamp in their room or make a cool smartphone case! Some projects or tools have age **restrictions**, so ask a trusted adult first.

Part of the fun of steampunk is to **tinker** with gadgets and machines and make new things look old.

ASK FOR HELP!

You might have to cut, glue, or take apart things to make items to add to your steampunk look. Because this can be **dangerous**, always ask for permission and get help from a parent or guardian. They may also be able to give you ideas for how to make your new item!

STEAMPUNK CONVENTIONS

Conventions are a great place to meet other steampunk geeks! At a convention, you can talk with fans and get ideas for your costume. There may also be vendors at the convention where you can buy more items to add to your costume or to your room at home.

There are lots of small and large conventions around the world. You may want to start by going to a small convention so you can see what it is like. The larger conventions will have bigger crowds, so they might be busier and seem overwhelming.

Many steampunk conventions charge a fee to buy tickets. If you want to attend, ask a trusted adult to help you save money and plan for the cost.

GOGGLES

Goggles are common in steampunk fashion.
You don't "need" them to be steampunk,
but they are popular at conventions!
Wear goggles if you like the look or if
your character is a pilot and needs to
have them. You can add items such as
cogs, fabric, chains, and other pieces.

Steampunk conventions, or "cons," can take place in large convention centers. Some may even take place outside! Some conventions have another theme, such as the Wild West. While there are many conventions just about steampunk, you might also see steampunk at conventions for other hobbies or interests. At comic conventions, for example, people may dress in steampunk clothing or there may be steampunk vendors.

Many steampunk conventions have educational sessions where people can learn more about steampunk or certain time periods. Some steampunk conventions also include a tea party, which is how the steampunk community first got together!

STEAMPUNK COSPLAY

Cosplay, or costume play, involves dressing up as a character, such as Captain America or Wonder Woman. Some fans like to cosplay a steampunk variation of their favorite character! For example, they may add cogs to Captain America's shield, wear goggles, or turn the superhero's outfit into a Victorian-style dress.

If you go to a convention, you might see a steampunk variation of a famous character from comic books, movies, or TV!

FUTURE OF STEAMPUNK

Steampunk doesn't show signs of slowing down! New conventions pop up each year. The people that have been involved in it for many years are happy to answer questions from newcomers and welcome them into the community. The steampunk community is accepting of the many interests people have and include those interests so that everyone feels welcome.

As the number of steampunk conventions, books, movies, and music increases, the number of fans interested in steampunk increases, too. This means you don't need to worry about joining the steampunk culture too late. Grab a cup of tea, hop aboard the airship, and join the fun!

ALWAYS HAVE FUN!

Creating a steampunk costume takes time. Make sure you have enough time to make your costume before the event that you want to go to. It can be overwhelming to think of everything you have to do for your costume, but don't worry! Remember to have fun in the process.

Over the years, steampunk has grown from a little-known hobby to a popular interest. Look and see if there is a convention near you!

29

GLOSSARY

appreciate: to admire and value something

convention: a gathering of people who have a common interest or purpose

culture: the beliefs and ways of life of a group of people

dangerous: unsafe

fascinating: very interesting or appealing

modify: to change some parts of something

overwhelming: when something is so confusing or difficult that you feel unable to do it

persona: an image or personality that someone presents to other people

restriction: something that limits or controls

science fiction: stories, usually set in the future, about how people are affected by pretend inventions in science

tinker: to try to repair or improve something (such as a machine) by making small changes to it

vendor: someone who sells something

FOR MORE INFORMATION

BOOKS

Steampunk Oriental Laboratory, ed. *Steampunk Style: The Complete Illustrated Guide for Contraptors, Gizmologists, and Primocogglers Everywhere!* London, UK: Titan Books, 2014.

VanderMeer, Jeff, and Desirina Boskovich. *The Steampunk User's Manual: An Illustrated Practical and Whimsical Guide to Creating Retro-Futurist Dreams.* New York, NY: Harry N. Abrams, 2014.

Willeford, Thomas. *The Steampunk Adventurer's Guide: Contraptions, Creations, and Curiosities Anyone Can Make.* New York, NY: McGraw-Hill Education, 2013.

WEBSITES

Airship Ambassador
www.airshipambassador.com/index.html
Airship Ambassador has information on steampunk events and articles on creating your steampunk look.

Steampunk Cons
steampunkcons.com
Steampunk Cons has information on all steampunk conventions and where and when they happen.

The Ministry of Peculiar Occurrences
www.ministryofpeculiaroccurrences.com
This website has stories and information on steampunk.

INDEX